Video Production Company

From Concept to Cash Flow

Table of Contents

Chapter 1. Introduction

Navigating the dynamic world of video production can be complex, yet endlessly rewarding. Our exclusive Special Report, "Video Production Company: From Concept to Cash Flow", breaks down this intricate journey into accessible, easily-understood steps. We invite you to delve into the nitty-gritty of launching your own video production enterprise, even if you are a novice in the field. We'll empower you with knowledge - from conceptualizing your unique ideas, managing budget constraints, to ultimately transforming your passion into a sustainable cash flow. Get ready to turn your creative aspirations into a thriving business! Our cheerful, straightforward guide acts as your roadmap to the promising landscape of video production. By the end of this report, you'll not only be bursting with ideas, but you'll also be equipped with practical techniques to make those ideas profitable! So let's roll the cameras, action awaits!

Chapter 2. Conceptualizing Your Vision

Every venture begins with a concept, a vision. The birthplace of any video production project too starts with a broad stroke, a seed of an idea, that if nurtured carefully, can blossom into captivating content. This chapter dives deep into conceptualizing your vision. It encourages you to tap into your innovative mind, refine your big idea, and set the stage for your video production journey.

2.1. The Spark: Identifying Your Idea

What sparks your interest in video production? Are there certain themes, subjects, or styles that you gravitate towards? Pinpointing your unique interests forms the cornerstone of your vision.

Ideation can be spontaneous or gradual. An idea might emerge from a single burst of inspiration or might reveal itself slowly, piece by piece. Whatever the process, embrace it! Don't punish yourself if a fully-formed concept doesn't emerge immediately.

Ideas could spring from a multitude of sources:

- Everyday life and observations

- Books, films, music, and other artistic mediums

- News and topical issues

- Personal experiences, interests or passions

- Client requirements, in commercial scenarios

If the 'spark' eludes you, consider brainstorming exercises like mind mapping or freewriting. Inject unpredictability into your routine to stimulate your creative process. Travel to new places, indulge in new experiences, or converse with a diverse range of people.

2.2. The Frame: Defining Your Concept

Once the seed idea germinates, give it a structure. Define your concept. This involves expanding your initial idea into a more cohesive, comprehensive format. A more defined concept allows for greater clarity as you delve deeper into the production process.

Think about the genre your video will fit into - documentary, short film, advertisement, or tutorial? What is the ideal duration? Rearrange and reorder your abstract ideas into a more defined narrative.

At this stage, it's also helpful to be aware of your target audience. Who do you want to reach with this video? Understanding your audience aids in shaping your concept to appeal to them effectively.

2.3. The Perspective: Establishing Your Point of View

Each video communicates a message, has a voice. This chapter segment explores how to fine-tune that voice. Which perspective are you operating from? Are you an observer or a participant? Does the video speak in first-person or third-person language? Identify and articulate what lens you are viewing your concept through.

Understanding the purpose of your video is crucial here. Is it intended to inform, entertain, persuade, or inspire? Aligning your perspective with the purpose will bring more resonance to your content.

2.4. The Blueprint: Developing a Brief

A brief acts as a guideline for your team to understand the goals and approaches. It should provide a snapshot of your project's objectives, audience, key messages, format, and desired outcome.

A detailed brief is like a lighthouse, guiding your video production towards its goal while providing enough flexibility for creativity. It should be a living document - open for revisions as and when needed.

2.5. The Sketch: Creating the Storyboard

Visual storytelling is the crux of video production. Crafting a storyboard helps visualize your video scene by scene, offering a pictorial layout of what your final product might look like. Each frame represents a specific scene in your video, including what's happening, the sequence, time of the day, location, characters, and camera angles involved.

Storyboarding organizes your thoughts and paints a picture - both literally and figuratively - of how your video flows from start to finish. It's also a great tool to provide a visual anecdote to your team, contributing constructively to their understanding of your vision.

2.6. The Symphony: Planning Your Audio

Audio plays a crucial role in enhancing and complementing the visuals of your video. It's responsible for setting the mood, creating engagement, and articulating messages. Plan your audio aspects early - will your video require voiceover or background music? If you are capturing natural sounds, how do you plan to record them, and what kind of equipment will you need?

Audio planning also includes scripting—documenting the words that will be spoken in the video. A precise script ensures your message is delivered effectively.

While conceptualizing seems like a gigantic task, breaking it down into these steps makes it digestible and manageable. This process, immersive and comprehensive, is as much a creative grind as it is an exciting journey of discovery. Stay open to ideas, flexible in your approach, and honest with your vision – the compelling video content that will ensue is bound to be worth the endeavor.

Chapter 3. Crafting the Perfect Team

Few elements hold more weight in the success of a video production company than the team you assemble. A well-chosen crew equips your enterprise with varied skills, innovative ideas, and collaborative energy. Right from the portfolio builders to the content designers, every individual will play a pivotal role. The coming paragraphs break down the process of gathering this creative cohort, ensuring you assemble a team that mold your ideas into reality, and helps your business prosper.

3.1. Identifying Key Roles

The organization of your team will largely depend on the size and scope of your projects. Yet, certain roles are universal and foundational in any video production company.

1. **Producer:** The producer is the driving force behind each project, supervising the entire process from conceptualization to post-production. They source funding, handle contracts, manage crew schedules, and oversee budgets.

2. **Director:** The director trims and polishes the vision for the project. Their job is to extract the best performance from actors and coordinate with the cinematographer to decide on the most effective visual approach.

3. **Cinematographer:** Also known as the Director of Photography (DoP), they are responsible for anything related to the camera: framing, lighting, and shot composition. They play a crucial role in determining the film's visual style.

4. **Sound Designer:** They work with everything auditory: recording on-set sounds, designing sound effects, and potentially designing

the film's overall soundscape in post-production.

5. **Editor:** Tasked with cutting raw footage down to the final product that reaches viewers.

6. **Visual Effects Designer:** If your production involves any visual effects, computer-generated imagery, or animation, this role becomes crucial.

3.2. Recruit Passionate Individuals

Passion fuels the long hours and the dedicated efforts your team will put into each project. Look for individuals who are driven by their love for film and video production, not just those who view this as another job. Their enthusiasm will translate into their work, bringing an unmatched energy to your projects.

3.3. Finding the Right Skills

Technical prowess and requisite skills are just as important as passion. Choose individuals who are extremely talented and skilled in their respective roles. While some skills are teachable, your initial crew needs to be competent and efficient from the get-go.

Remember, hiring for roles like Editing or Visual Effects will require you to put their skills to test. You should ask them to showcase their previous works or do a sample project for testing their abilities.

3.4. Ensuring Compatibility

Your team will be spending long hours together under strenuous conditions. It's essential to ensure that they can collaborate effectively, respecting and valuing each other's thoughts and ideas. Make sure their personalities and working styles are compatible.

3.5. Experience Matters

Seasoned members are an asset to any team. They offer stability and often assist inexperienced members with their insight, speeding up their skill acquisition.

3.6. Diversity is Strength

A diverse workforce brings multiple perspectives and ideas to the table. It could be diversity in terms of age, gender, ethnic background, or thought process. Embrace diversity when assembling your team.

Once you've gathered your perfect team, remember that nurturing them is crucial. Keep them motivated, provide growth opportunities, and maintain an open communication channel.

To summarize, crafting the perfect team is no less than an art. It requires a good understanding of individuals and a knack for identifying passion and commitment. This chapter provides you with a guide to assemble this creative force that imbues life into your projects and propels your video production enterprise towards success.

Chapter 4. Procurement of Assets and Equipment

The successful operation of a video production company requires significant investment in equipment and assets. Without reliable, modern equipment, your ability to deliver high-quality video content becomes challenging. The following detailed guide provides exhaustive explanations on the procurement process.

4.1. Identifying Essential Equipment

Before purchasing any equipment, it's crucial to identify what you will need. Depending on the type of videos you plan on producing — such as short films, documentaries, promotional videos, or personal vlogs — your equipment and asset needs will differ.

A basic video production kit usually includes a professional camera, tripod, camera lights, and audio equipment such as a microphone or sound recorder.

However, as your business grows, or the complexity of your projects increases, additional items like drones, gimbals, slider tracks, green screens, and additional lenses may become necessary.

It's a good idea to start with a basic list and add to it as your needs evolve with your business.

4.2. Research

Once you've compiled a comprehensive list of equipment and assets, begin your research. The aim is to determine the best value for money, without sacrificing quality.

Research can involve comparing online prices, reading reviews, contacting the manufacturer for additional information, and seeking advice from seasoned professionals in your field.

Remember, some less obvious factors to consider might include warranty offerings, purchase return policies, and the reputation of the manufacturer.

4.3. Budgeting

The procurement of assets and equipment is often the most substantial upfront cost for starting your video production company. Therefore, careful budgeting is crucial.

Categorize your equipment into 'essential' and 'nice-to-have' groups. Then, allocate funding based on these categories, prioritizing essential items.

Always keep an eye on your overall business budget, and be prepared to make concessions where necessary.

4.4. Procuring New vs Used Equipment

There are advantages and drawbacks to consider when deciding between purchasing new or used equipment.

New equipment will typically have the most advanced technology and be under manufacturer's warranty. It's a safe bet and is often reliable but can be costly.

Used, or pre-loved, equipment can be an economic choice, especially for startups with tight budgets. However, it can come with risks related to its condition and reliability.

To mitigate the risks, always ask for verification of the product's condition such as service transcripts or previous usage records, if purchasing used equipment.

4.5. Choosing Suppliers

Settling on which suppliers to use is a crucial step. Here, your research will come in handy.

Source your assets and equipment from reputable suppliers. Factors to consider include pricing, shipping costs, shipping time, vendor reliability, and after-sales support. Look at customer reviews and ratings as part of your evaluation.

4.6. Making the Purchase

Once you have decided on the supplier and the exact make and model of each equipment, it's time to go ahead and make the purchase.

Remember, procurement of equipment isn't a one-time event. As your business grows and evolves, your equipment needs will, too. Annual or semi-annual reviews of your equipment needs will ensure that you're equipped with the best tools for your video production company.

4.7. Managing Your Assets

Once your assets are procured, appropriate management is crucial to protect your investment.

Implement a system for asset tracking and maintenance. Regular equipment checks will prolong the life of your assets, and an inventory management system will assist with loss prevention.

Consider insurance to protect against unforeseen damage or loss.

Many companies also provide or lease equipment, and including protection for these in the contract will save potential costs in the future.

Understanding the procurement process is key to successfully launching your video production company. With sufficient research and careful planning, your investment in equipment and assets will propel your business from a simply conceptualized idea to a high-quality, lucrative video production enterprise. Let the reel roll!

Chapter 5. Understanding the Video Production Process

The video production process is a meticulous and multifaceted one. A successful venture into video production necessitates understanding how to create a roadmap to navigate through pre-production, production and post-production phases. Each of these phases consists of various critical components that demand your utmost attention and careful planning.

5.1. Pre-Production Process

Pre-production is the stage where all the foundation work happens for a successful video shoot. It involves a variety of activities like ideation, scripting, storyboarding, sourcing, and planning.

5.1.1. Ideation and Conceptualizing

Coming up with an engaging concept is the first crucial step in the pre-production process. Begin by identifying the goal of your video. Whether it's for product promotion, brand storytelling, corporate communication, or entertainment, clear objective-setting guides all subsequent steps. Once the goal is identified, brainstorm creatively to devise an innovative concept.

5.1.2. Scripting

Scripting is a significant part of pre-production. A script provides structure, and effectively communicates your vision to all involved in the making of your video. Start with a basic outline, followed by a comprehensive shooting script with dialogue, shot descriptions, and directorial notes. Scriptwriting requires a meticulous balance between narrative engagement and pragmatic execution.

5.1.3. Storyboarding

After finalizing the script, the next step is to create storyboards. Storyboards are graphic organizers that display images shot by shot with a description of each. These give a tangible visual dimension to your script and help all stakeholders visualize the final product, reducing miscommunication and ensuring everyone is on the same page.

5.1.4. Sourcing and Casting

Depending upon your script and storyboard, you would need to gather resources like talent, crew, equipment, and locations. Finding suitable actors for the roles, hiring an experienced crew, procuring appropriate shooting equipment, and locating ideal filming spots are integral parts of this phase.

5.1.5. Planning and Organization

Effective planning defines a successful shoot. Finalize dates, create a production schedule, ensure legal clearances for locations, and conduct a recce if necessary. Don't forget to prepare a shot list and a prop list to work effeciently on the day of the shoot.

5.2. Production Process

The production phase is where actual filming occurs. Every moment now costs money and time, making precision paramount. It's all about executing the plans laid out during pre-production.

5.2.1. The Camera Rolls

Once the set is ready, the camera begins to roll. Here, the director's role is pivotal. They guide the actors and crew, ensuring the scene aligns with the vision. Every shot has to be precise, capturing emotion, acting, lighting, and audio to create a perfect scene.

5.2.2. Lighting and Composition

Lighting and composition play crucial roles in the overall aesthetic of the video. They should complement the mood and tone of the scene, draw attention to significant elements, and present the visuals elegantly.

5.2.3. Capturing Perfect Audio

Good quality audio is as necessary as high-quality visuals. Pay close attention to audio recording. Ensure there's minimal ambient noise, the dialogues are clear, and sound effects are captured or planned for addition in post-production.

5.3. Post-Production Process

Post-production commences when you call 'cut' for the last time. Here, the recorded material is edited and polished into the final product.

5.3.1. Video Editing

The first step is to assemble the footage and start editing per the storyboard and script. This step involves selecting the best takes, arranging sequences, adding transitions, and refining the product. It's during editing that the story truly starts to take shape.

5.3.2. Sound Design

After editing comes sound design where all audio components — dialogue, sound effects, and music — are edited and mixed. The audio should flow smoothly with the visuals, enhancing the overall experience.

5.3.3. Visual Effects and Grading

In the digital age, visual effects have become an important part of video production. They can be employed to enhance visuals or create impossible-to-film scenarios. On the other hand, color grading enhances the video aesthetically, and ensures continuity in visuals across different scenes.

5.3.4. Finalizing and Delivery

Once you have the final version of the video, it's time to prepare it for delivery in the appropriate format. Whether for television, cinema, or online platforms, format requirements may vary, impacting audio specifications, dimensions, file size, and more.

In conclusion, the video production process isn't a walk in the park. It requires careful planning, creative ingenuity, technical knowledge, and a strong sense of storytelling. But with clear processes in place and a deep understanding of each phase, you are better equipped to navigate this challenging, yet rewarding field. The road to transforming your creative aspirations into a profitable, thriving business begins with comprehending this process in its entirety.

Chapter 6. Funding and Budgeting Essentials

Video production can be a costly venture, and understanding how to manage your budget is essential to the success of your enterprise. Here, we will discuss various key factors that play into the economic side of video production, such as devising a budget, securing funds, cost management, and return on investment (ROI).

6.1. Understanding Video Production Costs

Common expenses in video production can include salaries, equipment rental, location fees, post-production work, and marketing costs. Operating costs, such as utilities and overheads, are also key considerations. It's also crucial to plan for unexpected costs that may arise during production, such as additional crew needs or equipment failure. Rigorous accounting is crucial for maintaining control of your budget and meeting financial objectives.

6.2. Project Budget Preparation

Preparing a detailed budget at the start of your project is crucial to establish a financial plan. Start by listing all potential costs, breaking them down into individual line items. These can typically be grouped into categories like pre-production (scripting, location scouting, etc.), production (equipment, crew, etc.), and post-production (editing, audio mixing, etc.).

Remember, marketing yourself is an investment that can lead to more paid work in the future. Be sure to factor these costs into your budget.

For instance, the general framework of your budget may look like this:

Pre-Production

- Script development: $X

- Cast and crew: $X

- Locations and permits: $X

Production

- Cinematography equipment: $X

- Crew salaries: $X

- Food and travel: $X

Post-production

- Editing software: $X

- Music licensing: $X

Marketing

- Website development: $X

- Portfolio creation: $X

A detailed budget will provide an accurate prediction of your spending and help prevent unnecessary expenses.

6.3. Funding your Project

Knowing how much your project will likely cost gives you an idea of the amount of money you need to raise. There are several ways to fund your video production:

1. Self-Funding: If you have saved enough money or have a stable income from other sources, this may be a viable option. Self-funding gives you creative control over your project but also

carries the risk of personal financial loss.

2. Crowdfunding: Websites like Kickstarter and Indiegogo allow you to raise small amounts of money from many different people. In exchange, you usually provide incentive rewards based on the contribution level.

3. Investors: Private investors or production companies can offer significant funding. Such funding often comes with strings attached, such as partial ownership, creative input, or a share in the profits.

4. Grants and Subsidies: Several organizations provide grants for filmmaking. These are often tied to specific themes, regions, or demographics.

5. Sponsorship: Brands and businesses might agree to sponsor your production if your content aligns with their marketing or corporate social responsibility goals.

Each funding method has its pros and cons, so consider your options carefully before committing.

6.4. Cost Management

Once you have a budget in place and funding secured, ongoing cost management becomes crucial. Keep track of every expense and compare it to your budget. Regularly review your financial situation and adjust resources as necessary.

Don't be afraid to negotiate with suppliers to get the best deal. Wherever possible, try to minimize expenses by using cost-effective alternatives. For example, using unpaid interns or students who are looking for on-the-job experience in exchange for course credit could save pounds in crew salaries.

6.5. Return on Investment

Return on investment (ROI) refers to the profit you make compared to the costs of your production. A positive ROI means your production earned more than it cost, while a negative ROI means your costs outweighted your earnings.

Revenue may not be immediate, particularly if you're relying on film festivals, streaming deals, or advertising revenue sharing. It's essential to consider your ROI goals from the start and build a realistic monetization plan.

In summary, managing your funds effectively is as important to the success of your video production venture as any creative aspect. Proper budgeting, funding, and cost management practices will help ensure the financial health of your project and ultimately turn your video production passion into a profitable business. Understanding ROI will provide a practical frame to evaluate your success and guide your future video production endeavors.

Chapter 7. Tackling Pre-production Challenges

The pre-production stage is the foundation upon which your video production venture stands. To craft a blueprint robust enough to withstand any obstacles along the way, you need to tackle three core elements: conceptualization, planning, and budgeting - each presenting its unique set of challenges.

7.1. Decoding Conceptualization

In video production, an idea is your genesis point; it's where everything begins. But as spontaneous and exciting as brainstorming can be, it can turn into a minefield of indecision and confusion without structured guidance.

The first step is filtering your ideas. This is where you sieve through your pool of thoughts to unearth those with the potential to resonate with your target audience. This process requires a deep understanding of who your audience is, what they are interested in, and what they want. It involves market research, customer personas, and an understanding of the current market trends in video content. While tedious, the stakes of skipping this step are high, and it could lead to investing resources in an idea unlikely to generate returns.

Once you have the relevant ideas, the next step is developing those ideas into tangible video content. This requires scriptwriting – a challenging but crucial part of the video production process. It involves turning your raw idea into a cohesive story that can engage and captivate viewers. Scriptwriting requires creativity, excellent writing skills, and a deep understanding of storytelling strategies. Developing a solid script is vital as it serves as the guide for every subsequent stage of production.

Remember, a poorly written script can lead to confusion and miscommunication during production and potentially undermine the entire project. Hence, investing time and resources into developing a solid script will payoff in the long run.

7.2. Perfecting the Planning Process

After the scriptwriting process is complete, the next hurdle is planning, which includes storyboarding, location scouting, casting, and scheduling.

Storyboarding is the visual representation of your script and involves drawing out scene by scene what the video will look like. This process can be a challenge due to the need for precision and attention to detail. Furthermore, it demands a balance between creativity and logistic truth in visualizing what can realistically be actualized within your project's constraints.

Location scouting is the process of finding the perfect location for each scene in your storyboard. This involves considering factors like aesthetic appeal, logistic considerations, cost, and access to necessary facilities. It also often includes finding a backup location in case of unforeseen issues with your primary choice.

Casting is about finding the perfect talent to bring your characters to life. This involves holding auditions and choosing actors or voiceover artists depending on the nature of your production. It entails understanding the requirements of the roles and the ability to judge acting skills. Casting is critical as the wrong talent can ruin a potentially good video content.

Finally, scheduling; a task that involves balancing multiple schedules, including those of the crew, actors, location availability, and even factors like weather for outdoor shoots. Scheduling requires exceptional organizational skills, thoroughness, and the ability to anticipate and prepare for possible delays.

7.3. Battling the Budget Beast

After planning and scheduling, comes budgeting – a crucial part of pre-production that deals with the financial aspects of your video production project. Without careful budgeting, you may end up overspending and running into financial problems later on.

The first challenge in budgeting is estimating costs accurately. This involves factoring in the price of location rents, talent fees, equipment costs, crew salaries, post-production costs, and a contingency for unforeseen expenses. Underestimating costs, even inadvertently, can cause your project to stall or fail.

Negotiating is also a challenging part of budgeting. Mostly, you will be dealing with external parties for services such as location rents or talent fees. It's important to approach all negotiations judiciously, ensuring you get the best possible price without sacrificing the quality of your video.

Finally, managing the budget throughout the project is vital. This involves tracking all expenses, keeping them within the set budget, and making adjustments as needed. Having a strong sense of responsibility and organization is key in managing your budget effectively.

The pre-production phase is arguably the most challenging part of the video production process. However, with a good understanding of the tasks involved and how to handle them, you can navigate this phase successfully and set your project up for success. Remember, a solid pre-production will make the rest of your production process smoother and more efficient.

Chapter 8. Managing Production Like a Pro

At its core, video production management revolves around meticulous planning, effective coordination, and seamless execution. This chapter encapsulates these key attributes and gives you a comprehensive understanding of how to manage video production like professionals do. The succeeding subchapters delve into each component of production management in detail, from pre-production planning, forming the right team, allocating budgets, scheduling shoots, to finally post-production management.

8.1. Pre-Production Planning

Pre-production planning sets the stage for the rest of your video production process. It involves brainstorming concepts and ideas, scripting, storyboard creation, and logistics planning.

A solid script is the blueprint on which your video is based. It not only dictates the dialogues and the flow of the video but also serves as a reference for everyone involved. The next logical step is the creation of a storyboard. This visual representation of the video sequence helps everyone align their understanding of the script.

Logistics planning may seem like a non-creative aspect, but it is equally important in the video production process. It includes elements like location scouting, permit acquisition, equipment, and crew arrangement, talent hiring, and setting dates for shoots. Planning your logistics well in advance can save you a great deal on costs too.

8.2. Assembling the Right Team

The right team forms the backbone of any project, more so with video production. Determining your crew largely depends on the scale and budget of your project. A basic video team typically comprises of a director, producer, cinematographer, sound technician, and editor.

Depending on the complexity of the project, you might also need gaffers for lighting, production designers for set concepts, and a makeup and costume team. If you're working on a low-budget project, you might have to multi-task or hire multi-disciplined folks. Start with what fits your situation and scale as needed.

You would also need talent, which could be actors or voice-over artists. If your budget permits, a casting director can be invaluable to help select the right talent for your video.

8.3. Budget Allocation

This facet of management is perhaps the most challenging. Video production can be expensive, and careful budgeting ensures you produce a great video without breaking the bank. A basic budget should include costs for scriptwriting, pre-production, production, post-production, and distribution.

It's wise to negotiate with suppliers, crew, and talent to get the best price, but remember not to compromise on quality. Also, always set aside a contingency fund for unexpected expenses. Regularly revisiting and updating your budget throughout the whole process helps keep your expenses in check.

8.4. Production Schedule

Adhering to a schedule in video production not only saves time but also money. A production schedule outlines when and where each scene is filmed, ensuring seamless coordination between all parties.

Key elements in production scheduling include location, scenes to be shot, cast and crew involved, equipment required, and time allocation for setup, rehearsal, and actual shooting. Scheduling ensures that you fully utilize your resources and avoid last-minute inconveniences.

8.5. Post-Production Management

Post-production is where your video comes to life. It includes video editing, special effects, sound editing, color correction, and addition of music. Each of these elements greatly impacts the viewer's experience and perception of your video.

Managing post-production effectively involves having a good eye for detail, patience, and creativity. Having a clear communication channel with your editor, colorist, and sound engineer is crucial as they play a big role in shaping the final product. Remember, the ultimate goal is to maintain visual and auditory coherence in your video to engage your audience effectively.

Managing production like a pro involves a powerful combination of planning, coordination, and implementation. By mastering these aspects, you can transform your creative ideas into visually rich and successful videos. As you embark on your journey in the video production landscape, consider each project as an avenue for learning and growth. With practice and patience, the process that seems complex now will soon become second nature.

Chapter 9. Post-production: The Final Touches

Post-production is the last step in the video production process, but by no means the least important. In many respects, it's the stage that can make or break your project. This phase involves taking the raw footage shot during the production phase and transforming it into a complete, engaging narrative.

9.1. Step 1: Logging and Capturing Raw Footage

The first step in post-production is logging and capturing all of the raw footage that was shot during production. This involves uploading all the footage onto your computer or a dedicated server. Footage these days can easily be transferred digitally, though particularly large file sizes might require transfer via hard drives or even dedicated servers.

Organization is key here. It's recommended to create a dedicated file structure for your projects, categorizing clips based on scenes, takes, and type (like B-roll, interviews, etc.). You should also take this time to review your footage, far too often one rushes this process and overlooks potentially valuable shots.

9.2. Step 2: Video Editing

Once your footage is captured and organized, the video editing process begins. This is where you'll truly start to see your finished product take shape.

Video editing involves the assembly of individual shots into a single piece. Sequence the clips in the correct order, as outlined in your storyboard or script. Cut out unnecessary parts and edit based on the rhythm and the story. You can also edit to the beat of a music track, which often helps to keep the pace of your video engaging.

Remember, the goal during this stage is to convey your story or message as clearly and compellingly as possible. The goal is not to make use of all the footage shot; don't be afraid to leave something out if it doesn't contribute to the narrative you're building.

9.3. Step 3: Sound Editing and Design

After you've pieced together a visual narrative, it's time to focus on the sound. A video's audio has a significant impact on its overall quality and the viewer's engagement.

In this step, you'll edit and mix the dialogues, effects, and music tracks. Remove all unwanted noises using audio software. Retaining high-quality, clear sound is pivotal.

Sound design is all about adding depth and dimension to your video through audio. This can involve adding sound effects to enhance realism, putting together the perfect music track to enhance the mood and using audio transitions for smooth scene changes. The key to successful sound design is subtlety – you want to enhance the viewer's experience, not distract from it.

9.4. Step 4: Visual Effects and Graphics

Visual effects and graphics can take your video to another level when used appropriately. They can create an engaging aesthetic, help explain complex concepts, or set a certain mood.

Popular visual effects include color correction and grading. Color correction involves adjusting the colors in your video to ensure consistency and balance, while color grading shapes the mood and helps set the tone. Graphics can range from simple titles and text overlays to complex 3D animations.

9.5. Step 5: Choosing the Right Post-Production Software

There's an abundance of post-production software available, from high-end professional suites like Adobe Premiere Pro and Avid Media Composer, to more accessible (and often free) options like iMovie or OpenShot. Ultimately, the software you choose will depend on your project's requirements and your own comfort level with the software's interface and capabilities.

For sound editing and design, some popular options are Audacity, Adobe Audition, and Logic Pro X. For visual effects and graphics, consider software like Adobe After Effects or Blender for 3D graphics.

Always remember that while there's lots of software available, they're tools to assist you. It's not about which software you use, but how you use it.

9.6. Step 6: Quality Check, Feedback and Revisions

After you have edited your footage, worked on the sound and added effects, the video goes into an internal review. Be sure to review your video multiple times, check for mistakes, imperfections, and areas for improvement.

It's also highly beneficial to gather feedback from others. Fresh eyes can offer a new perspective and may spot things that you've missed.

It's rare that a video will be perfect on the first edit, so be ready to make revisions. Yes, it can be tedious, but remember these adjustments are polishing your final product.

9.7. Step 7: Rendering and Delivery

Once all corrections are made, it's time to prepare your video for distribution. This process is often known as rendering, encoding, or exporting.

When you're happy with the final product, you'll need to encode it in a format suitable for your distribution platforms. For example, a video for Instagram might have different specifications to a video for a TV broadcast. Ensure you know your platform delivery specifications to avoid any last-minute setbacks or quality losses.

Delivery of the finished product can occur in a variety of formats, including digital files, DVDs, or directly uploaded to a video hosting platform such as YouTube or Vimeo. Again, the choice of delivery format should align with the needs of your distribution platform and audience.

Post-production is a critical step toward turning your visual story into a polished, complete video ready to attract and captivate your audience.

While it can seem complex and time-consuming, every phase of the post-production process offers another opportunity to increase the overall quality of your video. Teaching yourself to enjoy the process, see every challenge as an opportunity for creativity, and commit to never stop learning will truly set your video production enterprise apart.

Chapter 10. Marketing and Client Acquisition

In this hyperconnected digital age, marketing, and acquiring clients for your video production company is both an art and a science. It requires a seamless blend of creativity, analytics, interpersonal skills and, above all, a deep understanding of your target market.

10.1. Understanding Your Target Market

Knowing your target market lays the foundation of any marketing strategy. It involves understanding who needs your services, why they need them, and how you can capture their attention. Begin by asking actionable questions. Who are the potential clients for your video production services? Companies looking for marketing videos, independent artists, non-profits, film agencies, or perhaps individuals in need of event videography?

You'll want to research the demographic and psychographic profile of your potential clients, understand their needs and wants, analyze their behavior, and identify their pain points. This vital information will guide the creation of your marketing materials, the sort of videos you produce, and the means by which you connect with potential clients.

10.2. Crafting Your Unique Selling Proposition (USP)

The video production landscape is often saturated, which is why it's crucial to set your company apart from the competition. Your USP encapsulates what makes your company unique, serving as a compelling reason for clients to opt for your services.

Here, again, understanding your target market is key. Adjacent to this, however, is understanding your own strengths, available resources, and how these can benefit your prospect. Perhaps it's your in-depth 360-degree videography, or your capacity to understand a brand's ethos and represent it visually, or perhaps your forte is quick turnaround times. Clearly define your USP and articulate it throughout your marketing campaigns.

10.3. Networking

Professional networking is a powerful tool for client acquisition. It allows you to directly communicate your USP, showcase your portfolio, and build personal connections. Face-to-face networking can take place at industry events, trade shows, business meet-ups, or local community gatherings. Still, in the current digital landscape, don't underestimate the power of online networking platforms. Linkedin, industry-focused forums, and social networks can connect you with potential national and even international clients.

Joining professional organizations can also help. These platforms offer networking opportunities, professional development resources, and often feature a directory where you can list your company.

10.4. Online Presence and SEO

The internet is typically the first place clients go when they need video production services. An informative, easy-to-navigate, visually compelling website can be your best promotional tool. It lets you showcase your portfolio, tell your brand story, list your services, and provide easy means for clients to contact you.

Search Engine Optimization (SEO) is equally important - it's no use having a fantastic website if potential clients can't find it. SEO involves using keywords relevant to your services throughout your website content, blog, tags, and meta descriptions, making your site easier to find on search engines. Local SEO is also critical if you're aiming to attract clients within a particular geographical area.

10.5. Social Media and Content Marketing

Social media platforms offer vast possibilities for client acquisition. They let you connect with potential clients, showcase your work, share behind-the-scenes content, tell captivating stories about your brand, and even engage with audiences using video content. Platforms like Instagram, YouTube, and TikTok are particularly useful given their focus on visual content.

Content marketing goes hand in hand with social media. This could involve blogging about video production tips and tricks, creating infographics about the process, sharing client testimonials, or writing about industry trends and news.

Giving away a snippet of your knowledge not only positions you as an expert in video production but can also lead clients who need video production services to your site.

10.6. Paid Advertising

With a well-defined target market and USP, you can also engage in paid advertising to attract clients. This might involve print ads in industry publications, sponsored posts on social media, Google AdWords, or display ads on relevant websites.

Be sure to monitor your ads, tuning them based on what's working or not. Online paid advertising platforms offer robust analytics, allowing you to analyze the impact of your ads and adjust them to maximize results.

10.7. Nurturing Client Relationships

From the moment a prospect contacts you, the relationship-building begins. By providing superior customer service, outstanding video production, and following up post-project, you can turn a first-time client into a repeat customer, or even better, a brand advocate who refers others to your company.

Follow-up emails, newsletters, and special offers are all ways to keep your company in the mind of your clients. Also, request testimonials you can use in your marketing.

Remember, there's no one-size-fits-all when it comes to marketing and client acquisition. Your approach will rely heavily on your understanding of your target market, your unique selling proposition, and the means by which you reach out and build relationships. Keep honing your strategy, stay updated with industry trends, and be ready to adapt your approach as required.

Chapter 11. Turning Projects into Profits

There's magic in creation, yet only when it translates into profits does the reality of running a successful video production company truly materialize. If you enjoy being creative but aren't quite sure how to spin your projects into a tangible income stream, this comprehensive guide will lead you on the path towards profitability.

11.1. Setting Pricing Models

Pricing is a complex yet key aspect of translating your projects into profits. There are several pricing models you can adopt, the chosen model would be contingent on the specific nature of your projects, your target market, and your overhead costs.

1. Project-Based Pricing: This is where you set a price for the entire project. Be it a music video, a corporate advert, or a short film, you identify the resources required, estimate the associated costs, and then add your markup. The advantage with this model is that it offers certainty for both parties concerned. Transparency regarding the overall project cost fosters trust with clients and helps them budget more effectively.

2. Hourly Rate Pricing: Alternatively, you can charge clients based on the number of hours you expect to work on the project. This method is particularly useful when the scope of the project is not very clear or can potentially fluctuate greatly. Be sure to account for production planning, administrative tasks, and editing hours when setting your hourly rate.

3. Value-Based Pricing: Another approach is value-based pricing, where your pricing reflects the value of the video to the client rather than the actual time or resources invested. This works best for projects that have a high potential return on investment (ROI)

for the client, such as large scale commercials or viral marketing campaigns.

11.2. Cost Control

Keeping costs under control is vital if you aim to turn your video production projects into profits. There are two main categories of costs in the video production business: fixed and variable costs.

1. Fixed costs: These are the costs that do not change with the number of projects produced such as rent, utilities, software subscriptions, and salaries of permanent staff.

2. Variable costs: These costs change with the number of projects. These include costs for talents, props, location rentals, travel expenses, and other related expenses.

Track every single penny spent to ensure that there are no cost overruns that can eat into your profits. Use robust cost management software to make this process less tedious and more efficient.

11.3. Monetizing your Skills

Apart from your direct projects, you can also generate income from teaching others your trade. If you have experience, there is no reason why you can't pass on your wisdom to other hopeful cinematographers and directors. Host workshops, run an online masterclass, or publish a series of educational videos for a fee. Using internet platforms, you can reach a global audience and create a significant new revenue stream.

11.4. Strategic Partnerships

Forming strategic partnerships with other complementary businesses can be a great route to profit. For example, partnering with advertising agencies, event planners, or even video raw footage stock companies, can offer opportunities for additional, steady income. Negotiate a commission fee or referral bonus for work directed your way.

11.5. Exploring Sponsorships and Government Grants

There are many companies out there that want to promote their brand in association with high-quality video content. Finding a sponsor can provide the necessary finance for high budget videos without the burden falling entirely on you. Similarly, government bodies and foundations often provide grants for video productions, particularly in sectors like education, public service, and the arts.

11.6. Upselling and Cross-Selling

Upselling involves selling a higher-end version of the product that the customer initially planned to purchase, while cross-selling refers to selling items that are related to those the customer is purchasing. For example, if a client is hiring you for a corporate video, upsell by offering a full corporate package that includes videos in different formats for different mediums (like social media) or cross-sell a package of still professional photographs from the video shoot.

Turning your video production projects into profits requires careful planning, strategic thinking, and astute decision making. As this guide has hopefully shown, there are numerous tactics you can implement to ensure the financial success of your video production enterprise. With this knowledge in hand, you're well on your way to transforming your creative passion into a thriving, profitable business!